PROJECT: STEAM

SIMPLE

SCIENCE PROJECTS

KELLY MILNER HALLS

Rourke
Educational Media

rourkeeducationalmedia.com

Before & After Reading Activities

Before Reading:

Building Academic Vocabulary and Background Knowledge

Before reading a book, it is important to tap into what your child or students already know about the topic. This will help them develop their vocabulary, increase their reading comprehension, and make connections across the curriculum.

1. *Look at the cover of the book. What will this book be about?*
2. *What do you already know about the topic?*
3. *Let's study the Table of Contents. What will you learn about in the book's chapters?*
4. *What would you like to learn about this topic? Do you think you might learn about it from this book? Why or why not?*
5. *Use a reading journal to write about your knowledge of this topic. Record what you already know about the topic and what you hope to learn about the topic.*
6. *Read the book.*
7. *In your reading journal, record what you learned about the topic and your response to the book.*
8. *After reading the book complete the activities below.*

Content Area Vocabulary
Read the list. What do these words mean?

balsa
camouflage
carbon dioxide
desensitizing
hydrogen
infused
molecules
optical
retina
saturated
shards

After Reading:

Comprehension and Extension Activity

After reading the book, work on the following questions with your child or students in order to check their level of reading comprehension and content mastery.

1. *What happens when you dissolve salt or sugar in water?* (Summarize)
2. *How does a magnet hold nuts and bolts through a piece of wood?* (Infer)
3. *How does colored water change the color of a flower's petals?* (Asking Questions)
4. *Is there iron in the cereal you eat?* (Text to Self Connection)
5. *Why does foam float on water?* (Asking Questions)

Extension Activity

Based on what you learned about the materials used in this book's projects, think about other simple experiments you could do. Research the ways different materials interact with each other, then develop your own unique experiment.

TABLE OF CONTENTS

NOW YOU SEE IT

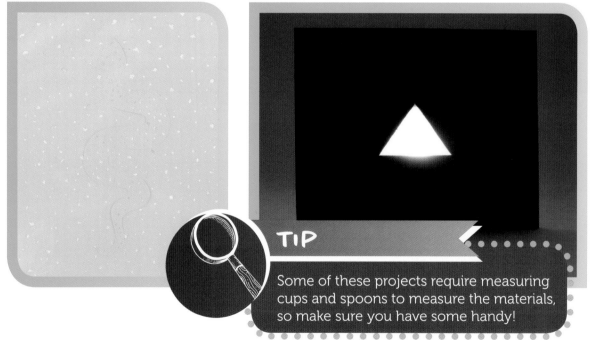

TIP

Some of these projects require measuring cups and spoons to measure the materials, so make sure you have some handy!

Is your breakfast cereal magnetic? Can you change the color of a flower's petals? And just how does a geode form? Gather your supplies and get ready to discover the answers to these and other fun questions with these simple science projects.

Disappearing Dot

Gather:

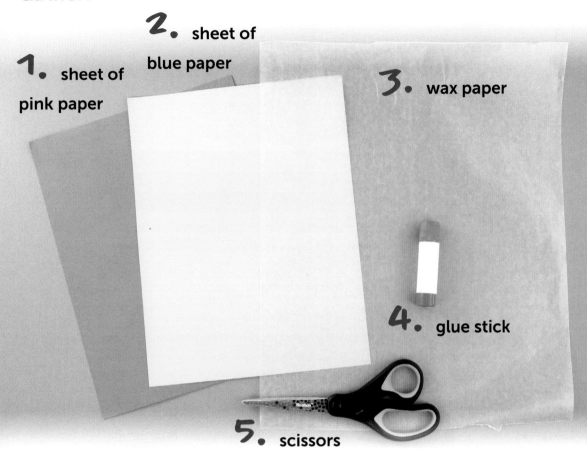

1. sheet of pink paper

2. sheet of blue paper

3. wax paper

4. glue stick

5. scissors

Do:

1. Cut a small circle from the blue paper.

2. Glue the blue circle on the center of the pink paper.

3. Cover the pink paper with wax paper.

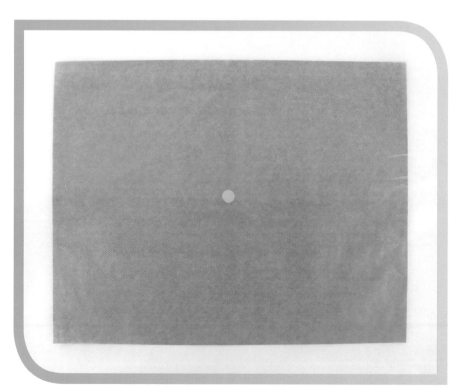

4. As you gaze at the pink paper, lift the wax paper toward your face and stare at the place right next to the blue circle. The blue will gradually seem to fade into the pink until it seems to disappear.

Try the experiment with different color combinations. Are the results the same? Increase the size of the contrasting color circle. Do the results change?

Observe:

The human eye is constantly in motion—tiny, jittery bits of motion. It's ordinary so we don't notice it. But when you do this experiment, those jitters create an **optical** illusion. The blue circle seems to disappear.

Magic Spy Glasses

Gather:

1. old plastic glasses frames with lenses removed

2. glue or tape

3. white paper

4. red transparent plastic film

5. blue felt-tip marker

6. red ink pen

7. yellow highlighter

Do:

1. Trace the shape of the missing lenses on the red plastic film.

2. Glue or tape the film into the glasses as replacement lenses. These are your spy glasses!

3. Write a secret message on your white paper with the blue felt-tip marker.

4. Scribble over your secret message with the red pen, then again with the yellow highlighter.

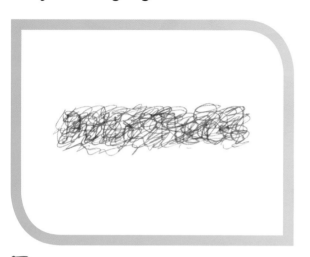

5. Put on your spy glasses and look at the message. Can you read it?

TRY THIS

Ask a friend to write a message in blue, then scribble it out with the red and yellow before giving it to you. Put on your spy glasses and read the message to them. Can they figure out how your glasses work?

Observe:

The red film in your spy glasses blocks the reflection of the red ink from your eyes, making the blue ink clear and obvious.

Hidden in Plain Sight

Gather:

1. two pieces of green construction paper

2. clear plastic sheet the same size as the construction paper

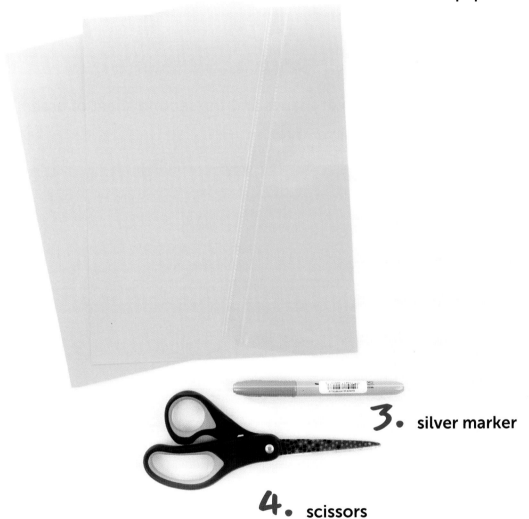

3. silver marker

4. scissors

Do:

1. Cut a snake or frog from one piece of green paper.

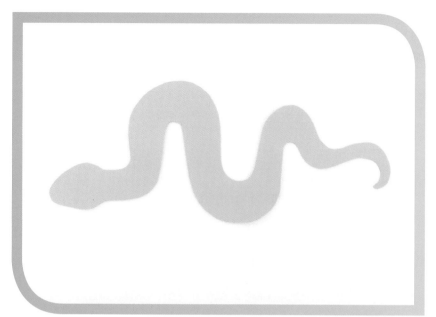

2. Decorate both the animal shapes and the second sheet of green paper with spots using the silver marker.

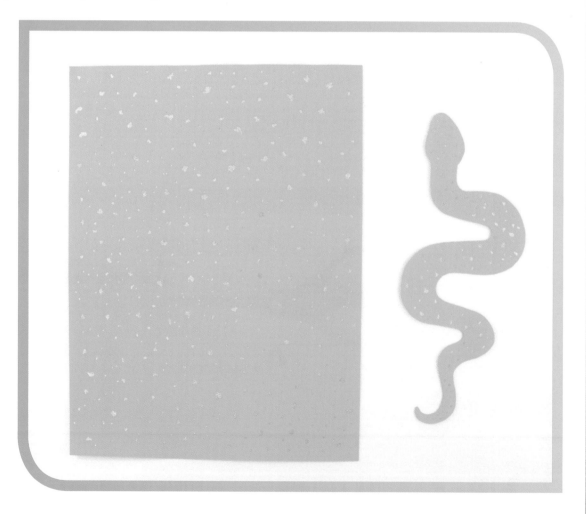

3. Place the animal shape on top of the spotted paper with clear plastic on top to keep shape from moving.

4. Stand six feet (1.83 meters) from the paper. Is the shape hidden?

TRY THIS

Attach a piece of string to the animal shape and replace the plastic sheet. Ask a friend to tug the string to move the animal. Stand six feet (1.83 meters) from the paper as you observe. What happens when the animal shape is in motion?

Observe:

An animal's skin or fur often acts as **camouflage**, helping them blend into their surroundings to avoid predators.

Afterimage Illusion

Gather:

1. 8 x 10 inch (20.32 x 25.4 centimeter) piece of cardboard

2. frosted tape (not clear)

3. flashlight

4. scissors

Do:

1. Cut a triangle in the cardboard and cover it with the frosted tape.

2. Turn the lights off so the room is dark.

3. Place your flashlight behind the triangle, blocking light from escaping any other part of the cardboard.

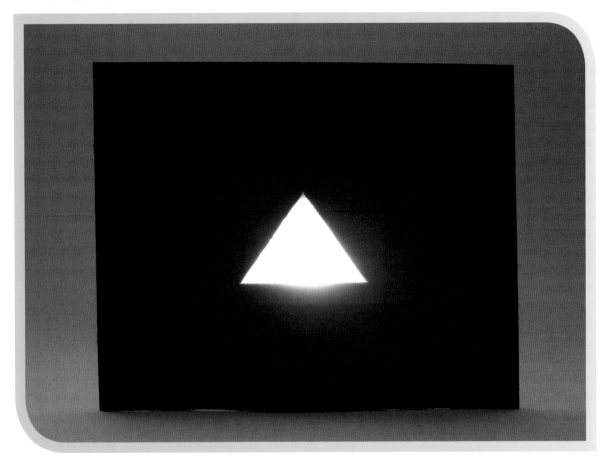

4. Stare at the light coming from the cardboard for 30 seconds.

5. Turn off the flashlight and stare at a blank wall. What do you see?

Observe:

The **retina** of your eye is its light-sensitive lining. When bright light hits your retina, it reacts by **desensitizing**—it adjusts to the light. When that bright light is removed, your eye needs time to go back to normal. If you stare at a blank space quickly, before your retina returns to normal, you may see the shape you saw earlier. That illusion is called an *afterimage*.

CRAZY, COOL, COLORFUL

No-Heat Lava Lamp

1. clear glass

2. one cup (240 milliliters) cooking oil

3. food coloring

4. 1/2 cup (120 milliliters) water

5. half of an Alka-Seltzer (with parent's permission)

Do:

1. Pour water into the clear glass.

17

2. Pour cooking oil into the same glass.

3. Add a few drops of food coloring.

4. Drop one half of an Alka-Seltzer tablet into the glass. What happens?

Observe:

Oil and water don't mix, so the oil stays at the top of the glass. Alka-Seltzer is a mild acid that also has a mild base. It will dissolve in water but not oil. When it reaches the water in the glass, the Alka-Seltzer's base reacts with the acid and forms bubbles of **carbon dioxide**. The bubbles in the water turn to blobs that float back up through the layer of oil. This reaction looks like hot oil rising in a lava lamp.

Cloud Burst

Gather:

1. water

2. clear glass

3. shaving foam

4. food coloring

Do:

1. Fill clear glass about half full of water.

2. Add shaving cream to fill the rest of the glass.

3. Drip food coloring on the shaving cream. What happens?

Observe:

Foam is a liquid **infused** with air so it floats on denser liquids such as water. Food coloring is also denser than foam. When the food coloring drips through the foam, it slowly releases its color in the water in graceful ribbons.

Color Bombs

Gather:

2. clear glass jar

3. 3/4 cup (180 milliliters) warm water

1. plate

4. 1/4 cup (60 milliliters) cooking oil

5. food coloring

Do:

1. Pour the warm water into the glass jar.

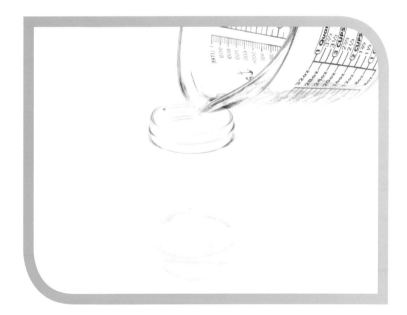

2. Pour the oil on the plate.

3. Add tiny drops of food coloring to the oil.

 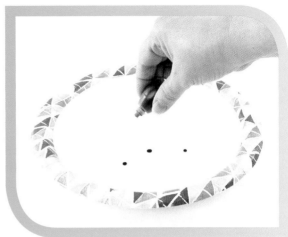

4. Pour the oil with food coloring into the jar of warm water. What happens?

Observe:

The warm water slowly melts the oil around the food coloring, releasing bursts of color.

Milk Makeover

Gather:

1. thick paper plate

2. dish soap

3. milk

4. four colors of food coloring

5. cotton swabs

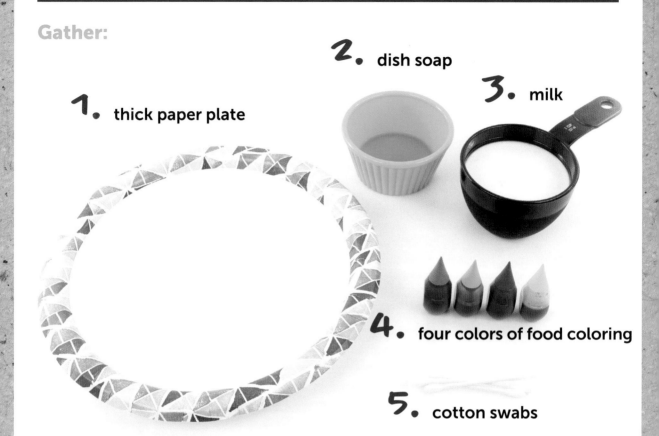

Do:

1. Pour milk into the paper plate—enough to cover the bottom completely.

2. Put one drop of each of the four colors of food coloring near the center of the plate. The drops should be close but not overlapping.

3. Touch the center of the milk with a dry cotton swab. Do not stir it, just touch it.

4. Place a drop of dish soap on a dry cotton swab and touch the same center spot of the milk, lingering without stirring for ten seconds.

5. Add more soap to the end of the swab and repeat.

Observe:

Water **molecules** love to stick together. Dish soap loosens that bond so the molecules flatten and mix with other fluids more easily. It's that property that makes it easier for soapy water to mix with greasy plates to remove grime.

Sugar Rainbow

Gather:

1. one tall, clear glass

2. bag of granulated sugar

3. hot water

5. measuring spoon

4. four clear plastic cups

6. four colors of food coloring

Do:

1. Put one tablespoon (12.5 grams) of sugar in the first cup, two tablespoons (25 grams) of sugar in the second cup, three tablespoons (37.5 grams) of sugar in the third cup and four tablespoons of sugar (50 grams) in the fourth cup.

2. Add three tablespoons (45 milliliters) of hot water to each cup and stir to dissolve the sugar.

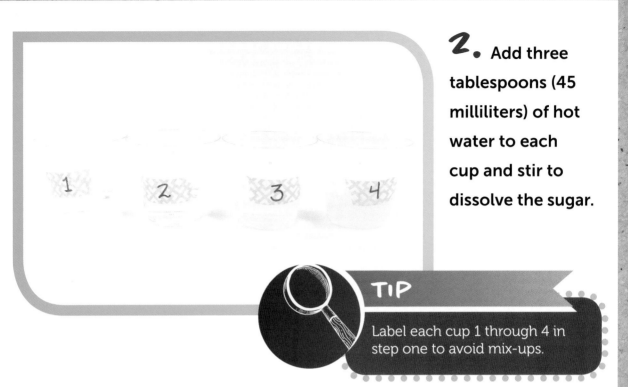

TIP

Label each cup 1 through 4 in step one to avoid mix-ups.

3. Add a few drops of food coloring to each cup, using one color per cup.

4. Slowly pour the sugar water from cup 4, which has the most sugar, into the tall, clear glass.

5. Repeat step 4 with the remaining cups, going from the most sugar to the least.

Observe:

Because each cup has a different amount of sugar dissolved in water, the liquids won't mix when slowly poured into one glass without stirring. So, for a time, there will be a sugary rainbow in the tall glass.

SO ATTRACTIVE!

Ironed Out

Gather:

1. clear plastic water bottle with a lid

2. water

3. iron-fortified breakfast cereal

4. strong magnet

Do:

1. Fill the plastic water bottle halfway with water.

2. Add crushed breakfast cereal.

3. Shake vigorously.

4. Set aside overnight.

5. Run a magnet across the outside of the bottle. What happens?

Observe:

When you run the magnet along the bottle, iron **shards** from the cereal will move toward it. But why is there iron in the cereal? Every cell in the human body needs iron to function. It helps the blood carry oxygen from the lungs to every other part. But human bodies don't make enough iron on their own, so we must get it from our foods. Meat, fish, and legumes are iron-rich foods. Iron-fortified cereals, milks, and yogurts also supply iron.

Soda Can Magic

Gather:

1. four empty soda cans

2. one 6 inch (15 centimeter) piece of thin wood (**balsa** wood is ideal)

4. strong magnet

3. assortment of nuts or bolts

Do:

1. Stack two soda cans on the right and two more on the left, side by side.

2. Place the piece of wood across the tops of each can tower.

3. Place the magnet at the center of the piece of thin wood.

4. Put a nut or bolt under the wood, directly below the magnet.

5. Add a second nut or bolt, then a third. How many nuts and bolts will the magnet hold?

You can try the same experiment with paper clips or small nails instead of nuts or bolts.

Observe:

The metal in the nuts and bolts is attracted to the magnet, even with a piece of wood suspended between them. How many it will hold depends on the strength of the magnet.

NEAT NATURE

Bottle Blow-Up

Gather:

1. empty water bottle

2. two cups (480 milliliters) vinegar

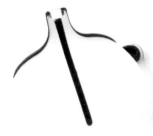

3. funnel

4. two tablespoons (30 milliliters) baking soda

5. balloon

Do:

1. Pour the vinegar into the empty water bottle.

2. Use a funnel to put the baking soda into the empty balloon.

3. Attach balloon to the neck of the water bottle.

4. Empty the baking soda into the bottle. What happens?

Observe:

Mixing vinegar and baking soda causes a chemical reaction. The **hydrogen** ions in vinegar and the sodium and bicarbonate ions in the baking soda form carbon dioxide gas that inflates the balloon.

Flower Power

Gather:

1. six white carnation flowers

2. six plastic cups

3. water

4. six colors of food coloring

5. scissors

Do:

1. Put 1/2 cup (120 milliliters) of tap water in each plastic cup.

2. Add 30 drops of a single food color in each cup.

3. Use sharp scissors to cut the tip of each carnation's stem at a sharp angle.

4. Place one flower in each cup.

5. Check every two hours to see if your white carnations have transformed. Keep notes on which colors change the fastest.

TRY THIS

Carefully split the stem of a single white carnation in half from the bottom to three inches (7.62 centimeters) below the blossom. Put each stem half into two different cups of colored water. What happens?

Observe:

Plants have a root system that reaches into the ground to find and absorb food and water. Cut flowers no longer have roots, but they do still have stem channels that draw the nutrients up to the blossoms. If the water they absorb is colorful, the flowers will reflect that color in their petals.

Jeweled Eggs

Gather:

1. eggs

2. egg carton

3. hot water

4. food coloring

5. salt (table, rock or sea salt) or granulated sugar

6. heat-proof coffee cup

7. spoon

Do:

1. Carefully crack eggs near the pointed end and discard the insides, then wash the eggshells with hot water.

2. Put clean eggshells in egg carton.

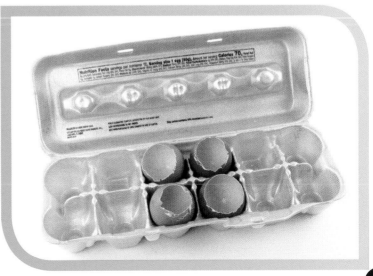

3. Pour 1/2 cup (120 milliliters) hot water, 1/4 cup (60 milliliters) salt or sugar and several drops of food coloring into the coffee cup, then stir until dissolved.

4. Fill clean egg shells with the mixture and wait.

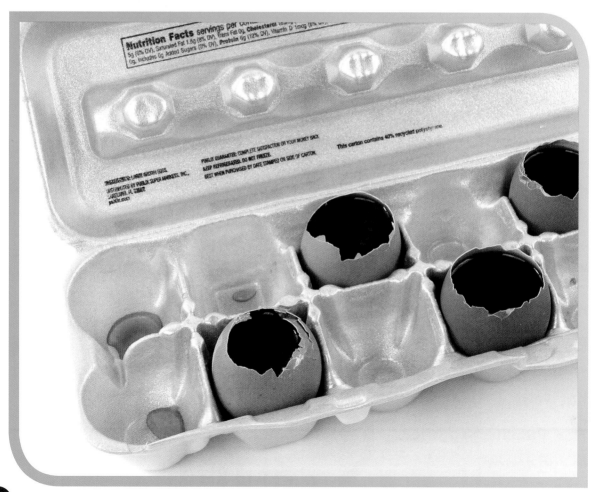

In a few days, once the liquid has evaporated, your eggs will be lined with colorful, sparkling salt or sugar crystals.

Observe:

Dissolving salt or sugar into water makes it a super-**saturated** solution. As the water slowly evaporates, the salt or sugar crystalizes. Geodes are formed in much the same way. Mineral-saturated water seeps into microscopic holes in solid rock. As the water evaporates, crystals form.

Living Leftovers

Gather:

1. glass jar

2. water

3. green onion roots

Do:

1. Add water to fill about two inches (5 centimeters) of the jar.

2. Dip the root end of your green onion in the water.

3. Place the jar somewhere it will get plenty of sunlight.

4. Observe what happens each day. Make sure to refill the water as needed.

Observe:

The rooted end of the green onion normally grows in the ground. But it can grow just as well next to a sunny window if you keep it watered.

GLOSSARY

balsa (BAWL-suh): a very light kind of wood grown in the tropical Americas, often used for model airplanes and rafts

camouflage (KAM-uh-flahzh): coloring, natural or manmade, that allows a person or animal to blend in to its surroundings

carbon dioxide (KAHR-buhn dye-AHK-side): a colorless, odorless gas

desensitizing (di-SEN-si-tiz-ing): making less sensitive

hydrogen (HYE-druh-juhn): a colorless, odorless flammable gas and the first item on the chart of Earth's natural elements

infused (in-FUZED): filled or mixed with

molecules (MAH-luh-kyoolz): a group of atoms bonded together

optical (AHP-ti-kuhl): related to sight

retina (RET-uh-nuh): a light sensitive layer of cells at the back of the eye

saturated (SACH-uh-rate-ed): holding as much as can be absorbed

shards (Shards): small pieces of metal or glass

INDEX

SHOW WHAT YOU KNOW

1. Why does soap mixed with water help clean dirty dishes?
2. Why did the red lenses reveal the spy glasses' secret message?
3. What happens when an Alka-Seltzer tablet is dissolved in water?
4. How does colored water change the color of flower petals?
5. Why is foam lighter than water?

FURTHER READING

Ardley, Neil, *101 Great Science Experiments*, DK Children's, 2014.
Heinecke, Liz Lee, *Kitchen Science Lab for Kids: 52 Family Friendly Experiments from Around the House*, Quarry Books, 2014.
TIME For Kids Big Book of Science Experiments: A step-by-step guide, Time for Kids, 2011.

ABOUT THE AUTHOR

Kelly Milner Halls is a writer who enjoys all things weird and wonderful. She explores life's mysteries in Spokane, Washington, where she lives with two daughters, too many cats, a Great Dane, and a four-foot-long rock iguana named Gigantor.

www.rourkeeducationalmedia.com

PHOTO CREDITS: Cover & all pages: © creativelytara;

Edited by: Keli Sipperley
Cover and Interior design by: Tara Raymo www.creativelytara.com

Library of Congress PCN Data

Simple Science Projects / Kelly Milner Halls
(Project: STEAM)
ISBN 978-1-64156-462-5 (hard cover)(alk. paper)
ISBN 978-1-64156-588-2 (soft cover)
ISBN 978-1-64156-704-6 (e-Book)
Library of Congress Control Number: 2018930488

Rourke Educational Media
Printed in the United States of America,
North Mankato, Minnesota